BRJC
9/11

D1175223

SNAKES SET I

COPPERHEADS

Megan M. Gunderson
ABDO Publishing Company

visit us at
www.abdopublishing.com

Published by ABDO Publishing Company, 8000 West 78th Street, Edina, Minnesota 55439. Copyright © 2011 by Abdo Consulting Group, Inc. International copyrights reserved in all countries. No part of this book may be reproduced in any form without written permission from the publisher. The Checkerboard Library™ is a trademark and logo of ABDO Publishing Company.

Printed in the United States of America, North Mankato, Minnesota.
042010
092010

 PRINTED ON RECYCLED PAPER

Cover Photo: Alamy
Interior Photos: Alamy p. 19; Getty Images p. 21; iStockphoto pp. 7, 17;
   Peter Arnold pp. 5, 16; Photo Researchers pp. 8–9; Photolibrary pp. 11, 15

Editor: Tamara L. Britton
Art Direction & Cover Design: Neil Klinepier

Library of Congress Cataloging-in-Publication Data

Gunderson, Megan M., 1981-
  Copperheads / Megan M. Gunderson.
     p. cm. -- (Snakes)
  Includes index.
  ISBN 978-1-61613-434-1
  1. Copperhead--Juvenile literature. I. Title.
  QL666.O69G86 2011
  597.96'3--dc22
                              2010012944

CONTENTS

COPPERHEADS

Copperheads are **venomous** snakes with sharp fangs! They get their name from their reddish colored heads. Like all snakes, copperheads are reptiles. So, they are vertebrates. Snakes are also covered in scales that are connected by stretchy skin.

Snakes are cold-blooded animals. That doesn't mean they're freezing cold! It means snakes rely on their surroundings to control their body temperature. They seek out sun or shelter to warm up or cool down.

There are five copperhead **subspecies** living in different parts of North America. These are the southern, northern, broad-banded, Trans-Pecos, and Osage copperheads. They are all pit vipers from the family **Viperidae**.

The copperhead is also called the highland moccasin.

SIZES

The copperhead's length depends on its **subspecies**. From nose to tail, Trans-Pecos copperheads average the shortest. They are 20 to 30 inches (51 to 76 cm) in length. Broad-banded copperheads are the next longest in size. They measure 22 to 30 inches (56 to 76 cm) long.

Southern, northern, and Osage copperheads are generally longer. On average, they grow between 24 and 36 inches (61 and 91 cm) long. Yet, these snakes can reach even greater lengths! The longest copperheads measure up to 53 inches (135 cm) long.

Copperheads are heavy-bodied snakes.

COLORS

As their name suggests, copperheads have orange, copper, or rust colored heads. The head is dark on top and lighter below the eyes. On some copperheads, a dark stripe extends back from each eye. But, the head isn't patterned like the body.

Brightly contrasting colors mark the copperhead's body. Its body ranges from pinkish to reddish to grayish brown. Its belly is pink, light brown, or cream colored with dark spots.

All down the copperhead's back are brown to reddish brown markings called saddles. These bands are wider on the sides and narrower across the back. They form hourglass or dumbbell shapes.

A copperhead's colors and patterns vary by subspecies.

WHERE THEY LIVE

A copperhead's coloring helps it blend in with its surroundings. It can live in a wide range of **habitats**. Each **subspecies** has its favorite spots.

Northern copperheads like rocky, wooded hillsides and mountains. People also find them near stone walls and on farmland. Osage copperheads enjoy similar habitats.

Southern copperheads prefer wetter, lowland areas. They often live near streams lined with cypress trees. Yet, southern copperheads also like fields and high, rocky ground.

Broad-banded copperheads also live near streams. They enjoy wooded or rocky areas. Trans-Pecos copperheads are found in dryer regions. They live in canyons and desert **oases**.

Copperheads are usually active at night. In cool weather, they may also explore their habitats during the day.

WHERE THEY ARE FOUND

The copperhead's favorite **habitats** are all in the United States and Mexico. Each **subspecies** is found in a specific region.

The Trans-Pecos copperhead ranges the farthest south and west. It lives in northern Mexico and western Texas.

The broad-banded copperhead calls central Texas and Oklahoma home. It also lives in south central Kansas. The Osage copperhead is at home in northeastern Oklahoma. Parts of Missouri and Kansas also support this subspecies.

The southern copperhead has a wide range. It lives from eastern Texas to southeastern Virginia. The southern copperhead lives as far south as Florida. Its range extends north into Missouri and Illinois.

Just like its name suggests, the northern copperhead lives the farthest north. Its range extends all the way from Georgia to Massachusetts.

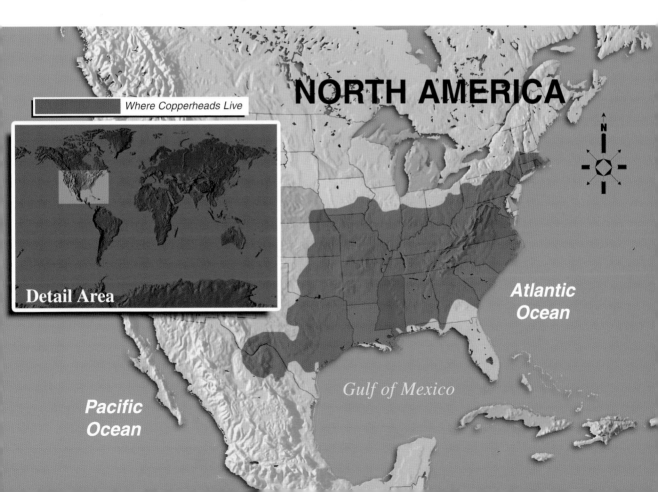

Where Copperheads Live

Detail Area

NORTH AMERICA

Atlantic Ocean

Gulf of Mexico

Pacific Ocean

SENSES

Wherever they live, copperheads rely on their senses to survive. Snakes have a hard time seeing things that are still. But, they can easily spot movement.

Snakes don't have **external** ears, but that doesn't mean they can't hear. Vibrations from moving predators or prey travel through the ground. The snake's lower jawbones sense these vibrations. From there, the vibrations pass on to the snake's inner ears.

Like many other animals, snakes smell through their nostrils. But snakes also smell by flicking out their tongues! The tongue picks up scent particles and brings them into the mouth. There, the Jacobson's **organ** determines what the odors are.

The Jacobson's organ is located in the roof of the snake's mouth.

Copperheads also have two heat-sensitive pits between their eyes and nostrils. These detect tiny changes in temperature, which helps copperheads find warm, living prey. This is why they are called pit vipers.

DEFENSE

Copperheads have to watch out for quite a few natural predators. Opossums, coyotes, bullfrogs, large birds, and even other snakes will attack them.

A roadrunner preying on a young copperhead

Human activity such as **habitat** destruction and automobiles also threatens these **venomous** snakes.

Camouflage helps copperheads hide from predators. The patterns of their scales create another defense. When copperheads are all coiled up, the designs make it hard for enemies to see their exact shape.

16

A copperhead's special coloring helps it blend right into its surroundings.

Staying hidden is just one way to stay safe. If a copperhead thinks it has been spotted, it may simply slither away. Or, it will shake its tail. On dry leaves, this movement makes it sound like a deadly rattlesnake!

As a last resort, copperheads will strike out and bite. They have sharp fangs that **inject** poison. This **venom** can be very dangerous to humans.

FOOD

Copperheads devour a wide variety of prey. Small prey such as insects, salamanders, and frogs are not safe from hungry copperheads. These carnivores also eat turtles, lizards, small birds, bats, rats, and squirrels.

Copperheads kill prey with their **venom**. They hide and wait for prey to wander by. Then, they strike out.

A copperhead has special glands near the back of its head that produce venom. This poison flows through the snake's hollow fangs into its victim. A copperhead releases most prey and follows it until it dies. Then, the snake feasts!

Copperheads swallow their food whole.

BABIES

A female copperhead gives birth to live young. Depending on her size, she will have 1 to 21 baby snakes at once. Most often, she has 4 to 8 babies.

A baby copperhead's length depends on the size of its mother. Most babies are about 7 to 12 inches (17 to 30 cm) long.

Young copperheads have bright yellow tails, which they use to lure prey. They are ready to find food right after birth. Even babies have fangs! And, their **venom** is just as strong as an adult's.

Soon after birth, snakes **shed** for the first time. Snakes usually shed their skin in one big, long piece! As they age, they will continue to do this whenever their skin gets too small or worn. Copperheads can live more than 20 years.

A young Copperhead's bright tail color fades with age.

GLOSSARY

external - of, relating to, or being on the outside.

habitat - a place where a living thing is naturally found.

inject - to forcefully introduce a substance into something.

oasis - a place in the desert with water, trees, and plants.

organ - a part of an animal or a plant composed of several kinds of tissues. An organ performs a specific function. The heart, liver, gallbladder, and intestines are organs of an animal.

shed - to cast off hair, feathers, skin, or other coverings or parts by a natural process.

subspecies - a group of related organisms ranking below a species. Members of a subspecies often share a common geographic range.

venom - a poison produced by some animals and insects. It usually enters a victim through a bite or a sting. Something that produces venom is venomous.

Viperidae (veye-PEHR-uh-dee) - the scientific name for the viper family. This family includes copperheads, rattlesnakes, and common adders.

WEB SITES

To learn more about copperheads, visit ABDO Publishing Company on the World Wide Web at **www.abdopublishing.com**. Web sites about copperheads are featured on our Book Links page. These links are routinely monitored and updated to provide the most current information available.

INDEX